GUIDE

MW01114310

Scouting and Civic Youth-Serving Ministry

Building Effective Scouting Ministry in Your Church

Larry W. Coppock, CFRE, Editor
The Reverend Greg Godwin, Contributing Editor
General Commission on United Methodist Men

SCOUTING AND CIVIC YOUTH-SERVING MINISTRY

Some paragraph numbers for and language in the Book of Discipline *may have changed in the 2012 revision, which was published after these Guidelines were printed. We regret any inconvenience.*

Contents

Called to a Ministry of Faithfulness and Vitality

You are so important to the life of the Christian church! You have consented to join with other people of faith who, through the millennia, have sustained the church by extending God's love to others. You have been called and have committed your unique passions, gifts, and abilities to a position of leadership. This Guideline will help you understand the basic elements of that ministry within your own church and within The United Methodist Church.

Leadership in Vital Ministry

Each person is called to ministry by virtue of his or her baptism, and that ministry takes place in all aspects of daily life, both in and outside of the church. Your leadership role requires that you will be a faithful participant in the **mission of the church**, which is to partner with God to **make disciples of Jesus Christ for the transformation of the world**. You will not only engage in your area of ministry, but will also work to empower others to be in ministry as well. The vitality of your church, and the Church as a whole, depends upon the faith, abilities, and actions of all who work together for the glory of God.

Clearly then, as a pastoral leader or leader among the laity, your ministry is not just a "job," but a spiritual endeavor. You are a spiritual leader now, and others will look to you for spiritual leadership. What does this mean?

All persons who follow Jesus are called to grow spiritually through the practice of various Christian habits (or "means of grace") such as prayer, Bible study, private and corporate worship, acts of service, Christian conferencing, and so on. Jesus taught his disciples practices of spiritual growth and leadership that you will model as you guide others. As members of the congregation grow through the means of grace, they will assume their own role in ministry and help others in the same way. This is the cycle of disciple making.

The Church's Vision

While there is one mission—to make disciples of Jesus Christ—the portrait of a successful mission will differ from one congregation to the next. One of your roles is to listen deeply for the guidance and call of God in your own context. In your church, neighborhood, or greater community, what are the greatest needs? How is God calling your congregation to be in a ministry of service and witness where they are? What does vital ministry look like in the life of your congregation and its neighbors? What are the characteristics, traits, and actions that identify a person as a faithful disciple in your context?

This portrait, or vision, is formed when you and the other leaders discern together how your gifts from God come together to fulfill the will of God.

Assessing Your Efforts

We are generally good at deciding what to do, but we sometimes skip the more important first question of what we want to accomplish. Knowing your task (the mission of disciple making) and knowing what results you want (the vision of your church) are the first two steps in a vital ministry. The third step is in knowing how you will assess or measure the results of what you do and who you are (and become) because of what you do. Those measures relate directly to mission and vision, and they are more than just numbers.

One of your leadership tasks will be to take a hard look, with your team, at all the things your ministry area does or plans to do. No doubt they are good and worthy activities; the question is, *"Do these activities and experiences lead people into a mature relationship with God and a life of deeper discipleship?"* That is the business of the church, and the church needs to do what only the church can do. You may need to eliminate or alter some of what you do if it does not measure up to the standard of faithful disciple making. It will be up to your ministry team to establish the specific standards against which you compare all that you do and hope to do. (This Guideline includes further help in establishing goals, strategies, and measures for this area of ministry.)

The Mission of The United Methodist Church

Each local church is unique, yet it is a part of a *connection,* a living organism of the body of Christ. Being a connectional Church means in part that all United Methodist churches are interrelated through the structure and organization of districts, conferences, and jurisdictions in the larger "family" of the denomination. *The Book of Discipline of The United Methodist Church* describes, among other things, the ministry of all United Methodist Christians, the essence of servant ministry and leadership, how to organize and accomplish that ministry, and how our connectional structure works (see especially ¶¶126–138).

Our Church extends way beyond your doorstep; it is a global Church with both local and international presence. You are not alone. The resources of the entire denomination are intended to assist you in ministry. With this help and the partnership of God and one another, the mission continues. You are an integral part of God's church and God's plan!

(For help in addition to this Guideline and the *Book of Discipline*, see "Resources" at the end of your Guideline, www.umc.org, and the other websites listed on the inside back cover.)

Scouting and Civic Youth-Serving Ministry
An Overview

the mission of The United Methodist Church is to make disciples for Jesus Christ for the transformation of the world. For almost a century, scouting ministries have been part of our concern for the spiritual formation of children in the Christian faith.

Scouting has been part of our reach to children and youth within the church and community since 1920, according to *Scouting in Methodist Episcopal Sunday Schools,* published by The Board of Sunday Schools of the Methodist Episcopal Church. This publication states: "Scouting is presented to the Church as a proved and approved weekday program for the boys of the Sunday School." Throughout the years, scouting ministry grew to include other youth-serving agencies. The 1948 *Discipline* (¶182) states: "Boy Scouts and Girl Scouts and similar organizations and clubs may be included in the church school...."

In the early 1980s, in an effort to strengthen the outreach to children and youth, the United Methodist Men, along with concerned Methodist Scouters (National Association of United Methodist Scouters), set a goal to establish an Office of Civic Youth-Serving Agencies/Scouting (OCYSA/S) ministries, with a full-time director. This goal was achieved through significant funding from local churches that served as a genesis in establishing an endowment through the United Methodist Men Foundation.

Since its inception in 1996, the General Commission on United Methodist Men (GCUMM) has continued its historic purpose as a lay movement "to win men and boys to Christ and the Church" (1948 *Discipline,* ¶1514.3). Today, scouting ministries in The United Methodist Church have expanded to include Boy Scouts of America (BSA), Girl Scouts of the USA (GSUSA), 4-H, Camp Fire USA (CFUSA), and our newest partner, Big Brothers Big Sisters (BBBS).

More than 1.5 million participants and family members are estimated to be affected by scouting ministries in The United Methodist Church. Scouting ministries provide local congregations the opportunity to mentor children and youth in the community in the areas of spiritual and character development through service projects, Bible-based resources such as religious-emblem awards provided by Programs of Religious Activities with Children (P.R.A.Y.), citizenship training, and by teaching new skills, connecting children to nature, providing leadership opportunities, and building healthy peer and intergenerational relationships.

Youth Agency Programs at a Glance

	BOY SCOUTS	GIRL SCOUTS	CAMP FIRE	4-H	BIG BROTHERS BIG SISTERS—UMM AMACHI PARTNERSHIP
TARGET AUDIENCE	Boys, ages 7–20, and boys and girls in Venturing, ages 13–20	Girls, ages 5–17, or in kindergarten through 12th grades	Boys and girls, preschool through high school age and beyond (1–21 years of age)	Boys and girls, ages 5–19	Boys and girls, ages 6–18
PRIMARY EMPHASIS	Development of character, citizenship, and self-reliance through small-group activity	Leadership development, service to others, skill development, and career exploration	Development of the whole child through goal-setting and problem-solving	Acquiring knowledge and skills for life, becoming productive in society	Promote positive youth development through one-on-one relationship with caring adult
PROGRAM STRUCTURE	Small group structure, youth interaction with adult role modeling	Small group structure with girl/adult partnership	Small group structure, youth interaction with adult role modeling	Structure varies depending on type of club	Volunteer supported in one-on-one mentoring relationship with child
SPECIAL FEATURES	Extensive drug prevention and youth protection programs, high-adventure bases	Contemporary issues series, leadership institutes, math and science partnerships, and GirlSports, a multi-faceted sports initiative	Community service, camping, and school-age child-care in addition to club programs	Variety of programs available, including national events	BBBS Amachi focused on church partnerships to serve children with an incarcerated parent
RELIGIOUS EMPHASIS	All four youth agencies recognize the God and Country series. There is a separation between church and state within 4-H because 4-H is affiliated with the U.S. Department of Agriculture. Other agencies encourage their members to recognize their relationship with and duty to God.				
NATIONAL OFFICE	Boy Scouts of America 1325 Walnut Hill Lane P.O. Box 152079 Irving, TX 75015-2079 Phone: (972) 580-2000 www.bsa.scouting.org	Girl Scouts of the U.S.A. 420 Fifth Ave. New York, NY 10018 Phone: (212) 852-8000 www.girlscouts.org	Camp Fire Boys & Girls 4601 Madison Ave. Kansas City, MO 64112 Phone: (816) 756-1950 www.campfire.org	National 4-H Council 7100 Connecticut Ave. Chevy Chase, MD 20815 Phone: (301) 961-2800 www.fourhcouncil.edu	Big Brothers Big Sisters-UMM Amachi Partnership 230 North 13th St. Philadelphia, PA 19107

Ten Reasons to Consider Scouting and Civic Youth-Serving Agencies as a Ministry of the Local Church

1. OUTREACH

The ministry of Christ revolved around the profound concept of reaching out to others. Modeling Christ's example, scouting and civic youth-serving agencies seek to touch lives with the compassion of Christ. We have found that when we reach out to others, the blessings of God are returned to us.

2. EVANGELISM

Statistics indicate that of all the youth who join scouting through the church, 25 percent are United Methodists, 25 percent are members of other denominations or faiths, and 50 percent come from unchurched families. Reaching out to families that do not have a church home is not a new concept. Scouting is one potential entry point for persons to join the church, which then has the opportunity to introduce, nurture, and strengthen the person's relationship with Jesus Christ. Scouting provides a great way for the local church to serve its local community and in the process offer new and exciting programs that the church may transform into ministry to, with, and through youth.

3. INTERGENERATIONAL

Scouting and civic youth ministry offers opportunities for older adults as well as youth. Often congregational members become isolated from one another because we tend to spend time with people of similar age groups. Scouting offers older adults a chance to become merit-badge counselors, mentors, or committee members who plan activities with and for youth. In these ways, and more, older adults can become an integral part of a youth's life. The experiences are ones that will be cherished for a lifetime.

4. COEDUCATIONAL

Some scouting programs exist for both girls and boys alike. Camp Fire USA (CFUSA) is coeducational for ages 1 to 21, while Boy Scouts of America's Venturing division is for boys and girls ages 13 to 20. These programs are a great complement to any church's United Methodist youth ministry and also serve to encourage older Boy Scouts to participate in scouting for a longer period of time. Girls may participate in many of the high adventure activities that boys do.

BSA Venturing crews offer a high degree of flexibility for their members. Some crews elect to focus on helping others through activities like building homes for Habitat for Humanity, while other crews enjoy the benefits of camping, hiking, and high adventure. Local BSA councils offer the use of their youth protection training and leadership training in addition to low-cost liability and accident insurance for their members.

5. UNITED METHODIST MEN

United Methodist Men groups have traditionally been the "standard bearers" of scouting and civic youth ministry. UMM units have been a source of manpower and volunteer leadership as well as a link between the church congregation and the youth agency. UMM have assisted in fundraising events, work days, special events, and a variety of mentoring opportunities.

6. MISSION

A variety of mission opportunities are made available through the five youth agencies. Camp Fire USA—through Gift of Giving, Teens in Action, and Extending Our Reach—educate and nurture children in projects that encourage their participation and commitment to volunteerism in a uniquely spiritual atmosphere. Similar opportunities exist within the various programs of the BSA, GSUSA, 4-H, and BBBS.

7. P.R.A.Y. PROGRAM

A study and award program offered by Programs of Religious Activities with Youth (P.R.A.Y.) focuses on discipleship, family, and service. Young people are drawn closer to Christ and are invited to become better acquainted with their church and pastor. The P.R.A.Y. series is a Bible-based resource that emphasizes service to others and brings recognition and increased self-esteem to the youth and teenagers who work closely with adult counselors and/or mentors. The P.R.A.Y. Program also serves as an effective outreach tool to youth agency members in the community.

8. DEVELOP SERVANT LEADERS (FRIENDS, FOLLOWERS, FISHERMEN)

Each youth organization includes "building blocks" that the local church can transform into effective ministry. For example, many youth-serving agencies require service projects that cultivate effective servant leaders. Youth start as "friends" (members of a troop or club), progress to "followers" of Christ (older youth who are setting the example), and culminate as "fishermen" (youth who do service projects to meet requirements).

9. INTENTIONALITY

The scouting program can be an effective outreach ministry of the local church. Through intentional planning, the church has the ability to transform these scouting programs into important youth ministries similar to other important ministries and initiatives. As a result, scouting always should be on a level with other church ministries. It has the potential to be a far-reaching, positive outreach youth ministry for the immediate community.

10. MAKE DISCIPLES

By considering one or a combination of the previous reasons, a local church may develop a consistent list of prospects for the Lord. Nurturing children, teens, and families through outreach and evangelism and incorporating them into the life of the church may have tremendous, eternal results for the youth, his or her family, and the Church.

SCOUTING AS A NEW MINISTRY

If you, as a church or scouting leader, are interested in using these resources to establish a new ministry to the community, contact the local office of the youth-serving agency of your choice. You will find them willing and able to assist you in the mechanics of organizing a program designed to meet the specific needs of your church and community. (See the Resources section at the end of this Guideline.)

If you have any questions pertaining to how civic youth-serving agencies might be used as an integral part of your church's outreach ministry, please contact the Office of Civic Youth-Serving Agencies/Scouting. Additional resource information is also available from P.R.A.Y.

Child and Youth Protection

the United Methodist Church and our partner youth-serving agencies have the goal of keeping every child safe. This is the job of every adult. Child abuse is the injury of a child by an adult or older child that might not be intentional but is not accidental. Abuse can be

(1) Physical—violent nonaccidental contact that results in injury. This includes but is not limited to striking, biting, shoving, burning, or shaking. Injuries can range from minor bruises to major injuries and death.

(2) Sexual—any form of sexual activity with a child or youth, prostitution, child pornography, and exposing a child or youth to pornography. The abuser may be an adult or a minor.

(3) Emotional—a pattern of intentional conduct that crushes a child's or youth's spirit, attacks the sense of self-worth, or lowers the sense of self-esteem through rejecting, threatening, terrorizing, isolating, humiliating, or belittling.

Child neglect is harm caused to a child or youth by withholding life's necessities, such as food, clothing, shelter, medical care, or education. Abuse and neglect are different situations with different dynamics but have the same consequence—the harming of a child or youth. Child abuse is a sin of commission, while child neglect is a sin of omission. Your local church and annual conference, as well as our five civic youth-serving partners, have child protection policies or guidelines.

Anyone working with children and youth within the ministries of our United Methodist churches is encouraged to become familiar with these policies. If these policies vary, the strictest policy takes precedence. If one policy defines an adult as someone 18 years or older, and another policy defines an adult as someone 21 years or older, an adult in your youth-serving group should be 21 years or older.

If you are aware of or suspect child abuse or neglect, please report it. Let your pastor, district superintendent, leader of your group, and/or the youth-serving agency office know of any possible abuse or neglect. These proper authorities will take the appropriate steps. Remember, reporting is not condemning; it is being responsible. Be prepared to keep our children and youth safe.

Big Brothers Big Sisters Partnership

Amachi

America faces the growing crisis of multigenerational incarceration creating a culture of imprisonment. We have already witnessed grandfathers, fathers, and sons waiting together in prison for the arrival of the great-grandson. There is a specific way that we as a people, and United Methodist Men in particular, can break this intergenerational cycle of incarceration. Research confirms the common-sense notion that the more caring adults engaged in a child's life, the more likely that child is to succeed.

Big Brothers Big Sisters (BBBS) is the youth-serving agency partnering with United Methodist Men to increase the number of men mentoring children with an incarcerated parent. Participation in The UMM/BBBS Amachi partnership requires the following:

1. Commitment from the UMM conference president
2. Support and commitment from the bishop and the district superintendent
3. Orientation to BBBS and Amachi
4. Partnership agreement with local BBBS agency
5. Selection and development of United Methodist congregations to participate in the partnership
6. Setting, meeting, reporting progress toward, and reevaluating goal of number of children matched to members of the partnering congregations
7. Sharing successful practices and lessons learned with other congregations, conferences, and BBBS agencies

See the national memorandum of understanding and a sample local memorandum of understanding at www.amachimentoring.org, and www.bbbs.org for more information on Amachi and BBBS. Contact the Office of Civic Youth-Serving Agencies, General Conference on United Methodist Men, for additional guidance. The BBBS Director of Partnership Development is also available for consultation and support (for contact information, see the resources section of this book).

Linking with the Local Church

in order for any of these programs or approaches to be effective within the ministry of the church, the congregation must become intentional in its use of the youth-serving programs. All too often civic youth-serving agency ministries simply exist within the physical facilities of the church, while the leadership of the church has little or nothing to do with either the program or its leaders.

The church should give the same prayerful and careful preparation to the planning of its civic youth-serving agency ministries as it gives to its church school or vacation Bible school. Properly used, these programs can provide an arena in which young people can have wholesome experiences with their peers, but this seldom takes place without planning and preparation. In short, the church must plan and operate the programs intentionally.

As the coordinator, you are the link between the church and the troop or club. You may be a Scout or club leader who relates to the church that sponsors your group, or you may be a representative from the church who relates to the troop or club. In this coordinating position, you will find that meeting regularly with the church council and the troop or club ensures that leaders of each group are aware of each other's concerns and needs. This Guideline will help you understand how you, as coordinator, relate to the church. Direction and instruction on relating to the troop or club will come from that youth-serving agency.

Your Ministry as Coordinator for Civic Youth-Serving Agencies/Scouting

first, take the quick view of both the marks of an effective coordinator and of the general responsibilities, then explore in further detail the essentials of healthy servant leadership.

An Effective Coordinator

- Understands The United Methodist Church and is encouraged to be a member
- Understands faith role modeling
- Leads and works with volunteer groups well
- Has a desire to grow and improve in the position
- Delegates work to others with sensitivity and understanding
- Has planning skills
- Communicates well with others by writing and speaking
- Supports people and their need to grow and improve
- Believes in service to young people
- Is elected or appointed by the appropriate conference (charge, district, annual, and jurisdictional) within which the coordinator serves (All local churches should elect or appoint a coordinator to ensure that young people involved in youth-serving agencies are recognized.)

Responsibilities of the Local Church Coordinator

- Interprets scouting ministry as an intentional ministry of the church, providing nurture, service, mission, and outreach
- Coordinates scouting ministries with other programs in the church and publicizes those programs
- Encourages dialogue and understanding between pastor or church leaders and adult leaders in the scouting ministry
- Is a member of the church council and reports monthly
- Sees that there is a signed charter or partnership agreement with the agencies
- Promotes the P.R.A.Y. religious education program for all youth in the church and provides information about the programs available for those of other faiths who are in our United Methodist Church youth agencies
- Works with the pastor in planning and observing Scouting Ministries

Sunday or separate special Sundays for each of the agencies that are represented in the churches
- Sees that leaders become fully trained for their positions in the agencies and by the church for youth protection
- Ensures that recognitions are awarded as appropriate, including the Bishop's Award of Excellence for units, the Cross and Flame, and Torch Awards for individual leaders, the Good Samaritan for youth who have provided service to the church or community, and other recognitions as needed, including public gratitude and agency awards
- Recruits Boy Scout leaders and leaders for other agencies, and assists in recruiting young people
- Assists the pastor with a report of the number of young people registered and the name and contact information of leaders
- Represents the church on the district scouting committee

Scouting Ministry Specialist (SMS)

The scouting ministry specialist (SMS) position is designed to help local churches consider scouting as a ministry, as well as a new response to one of the four areas of focus of The United Methodist Church: to develop principled Christian leaders.

The need for this position is based on statistics that only 6,700 of the 34,000 United Methodist churches have scouting units. The specialists will help churches understand the value of scouting and communicate information related to training, awards, and recognition.

Specialists will help provide information to the local church through relationships with the GCUMM office and annual/district scouting coordinators.

Specialists are recruited and registered with GCUMM and are responsible for up to three churches. They are not necessarily a liaison to a youth agency council/office like a local church scouting coordinator. Scouting ministry specialists are volunteers, so the amount of time allocated to the position is determined by the individual's schedule.

Qualifications:
- Must be 18 years of age or older
- Must present proof of having completed the BSA Youth Protection Training and/or Safe Sanctuaries and Sexual Ethics online course (offered at www.umscouting.org)
- Must provide an annual registration fee of $10 or $45 for 5 years to ensure that specialists will receive ongoing information

• Must read *Scouting Guidelines*
• Must complete SMS application, which authorizes criminal background check

SMS ROLES AND RESPONSIBILITIES

• Visit and communicate with up to three United Methodist churches in their area
• Assist the annual and district scouting coordinators
• Promote scouting ministry training events with adult leaders (Philmont, Sea Base, UM Scouters Workshops, etc.)
• Promote scouting recognition awards
• Promote the Programs of Religious Activities (P.R.A.Y) awards
• Enroll each church as a Shepherd Church
• Promote Scout Sunday
• Support the pastor
• Consider serving on Council Relationships/Religious Committees for the various scouting agencies
• Recruit one additional scouting ministry specialist

To become a SMS, please visit www.umscouting.org and complete the "Interest Form"; or call the GCUMM office at 866-297-4312. Someone will respond to your request with additional information

Faith Modeling and Servant Leadership

There is a difference between faith modeling and faith teaching. Faith teaching is instruction about a particular faith (for example, Christianity, Judaism, Islam, and so forth) or a specific doctrinal stance (such as one's beliefs about God or Holy Scriptures). The Office of Civic Youth-Serving Agencies/Scouting emphasizes faith modeling, while clearly stating that faith teaching is the responsibility of the home or the religious institution or organization.

Jesus constantly provided a faith model for his followers. When the disciples asked, "Who is the greatest in the kingdom of heaven?" Jesus, the ultimate servant leader, called a child into their midst and talked about becoming like children. Then he said, "If any of you put a stumbling block before one of these little ones who believe in me, it would be better for you if a great millstone were fastened around your neck and you were drowned in the depth of the sea" (Matthew 18:6). This passage conveys the high calling of those who inspire youth by modeling their faith.

As a scouting leader, you are entrusted with the precious gift of young lives. Parents, who have experienced the miracle of a new life, are sharing that miracle with you. They are expecting you to model your faith and to help their child grow. Civic youth-serving agency programs stress citizenship, character development, and physical fitness. These programs encourage you as a servant leader and are designed to promote these values.

Young people learn a great deal about their lifestyle by observing others and by practicing the behaviors they witness. Most parents can tell stories of how and when their children imitated them. Just as you have learned that personal skills are better taught by demonstration and followed by a chance to practice the skills, so faith development is encouraged by demonstration with encouragement and opportunities to practice faith skills. As a servant leader, you are expected to abide by the policy that specific religious instruction is the responsibility of the home or the religious institution. However, you can let young people know that God is important in your life by the way you live in their midst. You can live a faith-oriented lifestyle.

If you are a scouting leader in The United Methodist Church, you have committed yourself to holding a belief in God. You have committed yourself to a principle that says, "No person can grow into the best kind of citizen without recognizing his or her obligation to God." You have committed yourself to teaching young people both the words and meaning of the Girl Scout Promise, the Boy Scout Oath, or the Camp Fire Code. The best way to teach the words and meaning is to make them real in your life! If you are a representative from the church to the troop or club, you have also declared in your church membership vows to uphold the church with your prayers, presence, gifts, service, and witness.

What is faith modeling? It is doing, thinking, and talking out of a faith-strengthened stance. It is letting faith determine your lifestyle.

One aspect of faith modeling is respect for one's physical body. Inasmuch as civic youth-serving agencies do not allow alcoholic beverages on outdoor trips (teenage alcohol abuse is on the increase), a good leader will observe the practice of no alcoholic beverages, without exception. The same is true regarding other drugs and other health-damaging substances. Listed below are several other characteristics of a good leader.

A GOOD LEADER
A good leader will demonstrate love and concern for the young people in the unit, troop, or club. You will find opportunities to listen to them as individuals. You will learn to share their excitement, their joy, their sorrow, and their concerns. You will recognize that they have one foot in childhood

and the other in adulthood, hopping back and forth; and you will accept them for who they are.

A good leader will demonstrate the importance of his or her faith by being an active participant in the church, and that involves personal study and devotions. You may be the best model many young people will ever observe. Your faith life may encourage them to live their own faith commitments.

A good leader will foster spiritual growth by encouraging young people to plan and participate in religious observances during meetings, campouts, and other activities. You will want to plan activities to allow youth to participate in their own faith communities. Schedule programs and travel that will not conflict with such participation.

A good leader will encourage faith development by urging young people to enroll in appropriate religious-study programs. Just as young people need encouragement to work on advancement, so they need encouragement to grow spiritually.

A good leader knows that cursing is not a sign of maturity but is an attempt to disguise immaturity. Off-color stories or prejudice-loaded words will be avoided because they demonstrate a lack of value for persons (see James 3:5-12).

YOU ARE THE SALT OF THE EARTH!
Consider salt for a moment. Salt is inconspicuous and ordinary. Salt does not deteriorate, though it can lose its saltiness through adulteration. Salt is a preservative—remember that salted ham! Salt is an astringent that stings. Salt will stop bleeding! Salt gives zest to food and makes you thirsty! Remember that a pinch of salt has a great effect on its surroundings. When Jesus said, "You are the salt of the earth," (Matthew 5:13) he was saying that you are important. As a leader, you can live a faith-oriented lifestyle that encourages faith development in the young people with whom you work.

One of our bishops stated that he is a United Methodist today largely because of the efforts of his scoutmaster. When he was a young boy, his family was not active in the church. He attended one of two different Sunday schools, depending upon which of his friends came by for him on Sunday morning. One Sunday, the class teacher announced that he was starting a new program on the following Monday night and invited all of the boys to come back to the church. The new program was a Boy Scout troop. In a few short months this young man had advanced through the ranks of the Boy Scouts and had also become a member of The Methodist Church. In the bishop's words, "I joined that church because it provided me the opportunity to do the things I enjoyed doing." The scoutmaster provided the "salt" necessary to season the life of a future bishop!

A number of United Methodist pastors report that they have reached many families through the "salty" scouting ministry of their churches. One diaconal minister related the story of how a whole family was reunited with the church because of their son's participation in a P.R.A.Y. class offered by the church. The family had become inactive to the point that their name had been removed from the church rolls by action of the charge conference. The young Scout became so involved in the P.R.A.Y. program that he professed his faith and expressed his desire to unite with the church. As a result, his entire family was reunited with the church. Remember the words of our Lord, "You are the salt of the earth."

POSITIVE PEER PRESSURE
Traditional youth organizations bring young people together for regularly scheduled meetings and activities that help to develop a sense of identity and a feeling of belonging. Scouting programs offer the opportunity for youth to learn and grow by planning their own activities, electing officers, and practicing leadership. Leadership development happens unobtrusively and naturally.

While youth members of civic youth-serving agency ministries learn by doing in small groups, they are also exposed to the virtues of peer leadership and constructive fellowship. Young people feel the effects of peer pressure today more than ever before; consequently, it is the duty of the church to provide an atmosphere in which that pressure can become a positive force. Civic youth-serving agency ministries can provide such an atmosphere.

Relating to the Church Council

Your role as coordinator or scouting leader places you on the church council, where you will represent the issues of scouting and youth-serving ministries along with other church staff or lay persons who lead youth ministries. The following tips will help cultivate that relationship and help you develop your leadership skills and effectiveness as well.

- **Talk with the pastor, lay leader, or the Christian education person** about considering one or more civic youth-serving agency programs such as Boy Scouts, Girl Scouts, Camp Fire, BBBS, or 4-H.
- **Talk with your local church council** about community-based outreach ministries to children and youth in your community. Develop a plan and timetable.
- **Work with the committee on leader selection to nominate other adult leaders** for a Civic Youth-Serving Agencies/Scouting Task Group who will be elected at a church council meeting. Provide support for a budget. Continue the coordinator or committee positions through election annually at the charge conference.
- **Work with the Civic Youth-Serving Agencies/Scouting Task Group** to form a plan of action.
- **Report the plan and timetables to the church council** for input, approval, and implementation.
- **Survey the church and community** to assess interest as to what type(s) of unit or troops could or should be formed from Camp Fire, Girl Scout, or Boy Scout groups. Consider starting a mentoring ministry like Amachi, a program of BBBS.
- **Contact the appropriate local civic youth-serving agency** to get its professional help in forming units, troops, clubs, or mentoring programs.
- **Schedule a children and youth recruiting night.** Draft an agenda, secure leaders, organize units and troops, and set meeting dates. Let this become a night for Civic Youth-Serving Agencies/Scouting Ministries.
- **Form needed units and troops** that will be supported by the church and community.
- **Report success to the church council.** Set a date for a Civic Youth-Serving Agencies/Scouting Ministries Sunday worship celebration. Have a consecration service for leaders.

Events and Programs

Bishop's Dinner for Scouting

One of the most successful methods of helping local congregations understand the potential of civic youth-serving ministry within our Church is the
Bishop's Dinner. These dinners have been held in many annual conferences
at both the conference and district level.

PURPOSE

A Bishop's Dinner for Scouting brings together representatives from a number of United Methodist congregations at the invitation of the bishop. The
purpose of this dinner is twofold. First, the dinner affords conference leaders the opportunity to help local congregations understand how their youth-
serving program can become an integral part of the ministry and life of the
church. Second, the dinner provides an excellent forum to showcase the programs offered by the five youth-serving agencies and to encourage local
congregations to incorporate one or more of them into their ministry.

PLANNING AND EXECUTION

The initiation of a Bishop's Dinner can come from the Conference Scouting
Committee or the local office of one of the youth-serving agencies. In all
cases it is mandatory that the program be developed through the conference
scouting coordinator, conference men's president, and in cooperation with
the conference director of connectional ministries. In planning the program,
it will be necessary to determine whether to include the entire conference or
to limit the effort to a district or group of districts. These dinners should
include all five youth-serving agencies.

To ensure success, at least three months' lead time should be provided for
the proper planning and organization of the program. A publication offering
guidelines for organizing a United Methodist Bishop's Dinner for scouting
is available from the Office of Civic Youth-Serving Agencies/Scouting in
Nashville.

P.R.A.Y. Program

The P.R.A.Y. Program is a discipleship and outreach resource. It is also the
religious recognition program designed for use by the Boy Scouts of
America, Girl Scouts of the USA, and Camp Fire USA. (Church and state
issues may affect participation through 4-H since it is administered through
the Department of Agriculture.) Congregations have used the P.R.A.Y. curriculum in their Sunday school classes, vacation Bible schools, confirmation
classes, and other small group settings in addition to using it as an outreach

program to scouting groups in the community. To earn this award, youth need to complete the requirements in the student workbook under the supervision of a counselor (either the pastor or someone appointed by the pastor). There are four programs. Each program has its own Student Workbook, Counselor Manual, and Adult Mentor Workbook.

GOD AND ME (GRADES 1–3)

The God and Me curriculum is designed to help children become best friends with Jesus and tell their story of "God and Me" together. Children will make a game in each lesson and keep their games in a GAMEBox (God and Me Exploring Box). These games will reinforce the Bible lessons and provide opportunities for families to explore God's love together. There are four lessons:

1. God Created Me
2. Jesus Is God's Gift to Me
3. I Can Talk with God
4. Because God Cares for Me, I Can Care for Others

GOD AND FAMILY (GRADES 4–5)

The God and Family curriculum is designed to help youth understand the importance of family and God's role in a healthy family. Families may be compared to pizza: the layers of a pizza illustrate God's plan for strengthening families. Students will make a pizza as they study how families can grow together in God's love, and they will choose "family projects" to be done with their family at home.

1. Crust-Foundation—We are God's Family
2. Sauce—Family Heritage, Spiritual Heritage
3. Toppings—Our Talents and Gifts Strengthen Our Families
4. Cheese—In God's Family We're Loved No Matter What! Because We're Loved, We Follow Rules
5. Bake—Being in God's Family Helps Us When Things Are Tough
6. Eat, Share, Enjoy!—In God's Family, We Share as a Response to God's Love

GOD AND CHURCH (GRADES 6–8)

The God and Church program will lead young people on a journey. It will be a faith journey with three parts: meeting Jesus, worshiping God, and witnessing and ministering for Christ. Participants will create either a video or a photo album to share what they have learned on their faith journeys. Young people will have the opportunity to work with their pastor or other Christian adult as they study the Church's structures and objectives and participate in service projects that will give them a better understanding of the mission of the Church.

My Journey: Meeting Christ
1. Meeting Jesus, the Person
2. Meeting Jesus, the Son of God
3. Meeting Jesus, the Head of the Church
Project: Daily Bible Reading

My Journey: Worshiping God
4. Learning How Christ Worshiped God
5. Exploring How My Congregation Worships God
Project: Discovering How I Can Worship God

My Journey: Witnessing and Ministering for Christ
6. Learning How Christ Witnessed and Ministered to Others
7. Exploring How My Congregation Witnesses and Ministers to Others
Project: Discovering How I Can Witness and Minister to Others

GOD AND LIFE (GRADES 9–12)

The God and Life program will help students understand their call to discipleship. The curriculum focuses on the life of the apostle Paul as recorded in Acts 9:1-31. This brief account describes how Paul encountered Christ and was changed forever. Five chronological "events" from this story will be highlighted and used as the focus for the five different sections in this program. Each section will illustrate a key element in learning how to live one's life for Christ:
1. God Calls All Kinds of People
2. God Doesn't Expect Us to Do It on Our Own
3. Each of Us Must Make a Personal Response to the Call of God
4. God Gives Strength to Face Adversities
5. God Can Accomplish Great Things Through Those Who Are Willing to Do God's Will

P.R.A.Y. Mentor Program

The P.R.A.Y. Mentor Program for adults is designed for parents to work side-by-side with their children sharing in the work of the P.R.A.Y. Program. As the child examines his or her faith, the parent will be there, learning about God's love, sharing new experiences, and making discoveries with the child. To participate in this program, parents need a copy of the Mentor Workbook, and they need to work under the supervision of the pastor (or someone appointed by the pastor). Please note that the adult mentor does not take the place of the counselor.

P.R.A.Y. RESOURCES

Visit the P.R.A.Y. website at www.praypub.org to view the P.R.A.Y. Start-up Kit, PowerPoint presentations, sample lessons, and other important resources. You can also sign up to receive the *P.R.A.Y. News Bulletin*.

AFFIRMATION OF FAITH
Written by the God and Church Class
Evansville District Boy Scout, Girl Scout and Camp
Fire Retreat
Camp Santa Claus
February 18–20, 2000

Faith is not something you can see.
Rather it is something you know and feel.
Whether your faith is the size of a mustard seed or the size of a mountain,
You need faith.

I believe faith is like a mustard seed.
You believe a little when the seed is planted.
As the seed grows, so does your faith.
It will never stop.

In the past, God started us out
And now he is just trying to keep us going in our faith.
We have our faith in Christ.
We believe in Christ.
He died for us.
His teachings are so strong that they have lasted for years.

I believe Jesus is the Son of God.
God is almighty, all powerful, all seeing and all loving.
If you believe in the Lord Jesus Christ,
You will live forever in the company of angels.

A light in the darkness, a face in the crowd.
Faith is what is there when there's no one around.

(Authors: Emily Wuchner, Ann Ferguson, Ryan Grossman, Britteny McDaniel, Mallory Fuhs, Chip Peace, Sean Mabrey, and Stacie Keevil)

It is most important that we properly recognize those who give their time and talents to make the civic youth-serving agency ministry possible. This ministry can no more function without volunteer leadership than could the Sunday school or any other branch of the Church's ministry. It is also fitting and proper to recognize levels of performance that surpass the ordinary. Several awards and recognition programs have been developed for this purpose.

Recognitions and Awards

i t is important that we recognize those who make the civic youth-serving agency ministry possible. Volunteer leadership is vital just as in any other branch of the Church's ministry. Several awards and recognition programs have been developed to recognize levels of performance that surpass the ordinary. Applications and reference materials can be found at www.umcscouting.org.

Complete information relating to all of these awards is available through the Office of Civic Youth-Serving Agencies/Scouting at the General Commission on United Methodist Men in Nashville, Tennessee. (The brochures can be downloaded from www.umscouting.org.)

The Bishop's Award of Excellence

The Bishop's Award of Excellence (BAE) recognizes congregations and units within The United Methodist Church that extend their ministry to children and youth by creating a faith-based environment for children, youth, their families, and their leaders to participate in the following civic youth-serving agencies: Boy Scouts of America, Girl Scouts of the USA, and Camp Fire USA.

BAE was revised in 2007 and requires the election of a local scouting coordinator by the local church, the promotion and use of the P.R.A.Y. religious emblem programs, celebration of the ministry, and encourages the use of signed partnership agreements (¶256.4a, the *Book of Discipline*). See the application for the complete criteria. The Bishop's Award of Excellence is authorized for the purpose of recognizing outstanding United Methodist Church troops, units, or clubs that have met the established criteria.

Upon nomination by the local scouting coordinator and approval by a proper committee or representative of the annual conference, the Bishop's Award of Excellence is presented by the presiding bishop to the pastor, the unit leader, and at least one member of the unit at the next regular session of the annual conference. The BAE application should be forwarded from the local congregation at least six to eight weeks before the annual conference session. The award recognizes activity of one year and may be earned again.

The Cross and Flame Award

The Cross and Flame Award gives recognition to adult leaders who have given exceptional service in the use and promotion of scouting ministries for young people.
The Cross and Flame Award is awarded by the local congregation. The

award is authorized for recognizing leaders with outstanding service to youth at the local church level. In order to qualify, a person must have been an active adult leader in a youth-serving agency for at least three years (that is, Boy Scouts, Girl Scouts, BBBS, or Camp Fire). The candidate must also be an active member of a recognized Christian church.

The Torch Award

The Torch Award recognizes adult leaders who have given exceptional service in the use and promotion of scouting ministries beyond the local church.

Presented by the annual conference, the award recognizes adult leaders with outstanding service to youth at the annual conference level. In order to qualify, a person must be an active member of The United Methodist Church who has given four years of outstanding leadership to children and youth through one of the youth-serving agency programs (Boy Scouts, Girl Scouts, BBBS, or Camp Fire) and must be nominated for the award.

The Silver Torch Award

The Silver Torch may be awarded to an adult for exemplary service to scouting and/or youth ministry beyond the annual conference. The award may be presented to an individual who has served at the central conference (international), general church (national) or jurisdictional (regional) levels.

Unlike the Cross and Flame and the Torch awards, the Silver Torch has no tenure requirement. Recipients must be Christian but not necessarily a member of The United Methodist Church.

Examples of service include the following: (1) Candidates may be leaders of the BSA National Jamboree or International Jamboree; (2) Candidates may have provided leadership for mission trips to a central conference, or perhaps they directed efforts to raise funds to support central conference evangelistic initiatives for youth and/or scouting; (3) Nominees may have performed significant acts of mission and/or ministry in response to the Connectional Table areas of collaboration supported and advocated by the general agencies: (a) leadership development, (b) new church development, (c) global health, and (d) the elimination of poverty.

The Good Samaritan Award

The Good Samaritan Award is based on the attributes of the parable of the good Samaritan, Luke 10:25-37, and our responsibility as Christians to reach out to people in need of a "helping hand" as exemplified by the good Samaritan and related to us in various passages in the Gospels.

The purpose of this award is to recognize individual youth who demonstrate the attributes of servant leadership to others through outreach, humanitarian assistance, or advocacy.

The youth candidate must be a registered member of a civic youth-serving agency unit (Boy Scout troop, Girl Scout troop, Venture crew, or Camp Fire club) meeting in or chartered/sponsored by a United Methodist church; or an active member of a United Methodist Youth Fellowship; or an active youth member of a United Methodist congregation. Candidates must be between the ages of 6 and 30 (not yet reached 31st birthday). Recipients may be participants in an outreach ministry of a local United Methodist church giving the award. It is not necessary for them to be members of the denomination.

The Shepherd Church Charter Recognition

Shepherd Church Charter Recognition

authorized by

THE GENERAL COMMISSION ON UNITED METHODIST MEN

of

THE UNITED METHODIST CHURCH

is presented to

*in recognition of outstanding accomplishments
in fulfilling the established criteria.*

Given this _____ day of _____, _____

*"Train a child in the way he should go
and when he is old he will not turn from it."*
Proverbs 22:6

General Secretary
GCUMM

National Director
Civic Youth–Serving Agencies/Scouting GCUMM

The Shepherd Church Charter Recognition is given to annually recognize churches that provide outstanding ministry to their communities through sponsorship of one or more of the following civic youth-serving agencies: Boy Scouts of America, Girl Scouts of the USA, Camp Fire USA, and/or Big Brothers Big Sisters. These churches welcome all youth and children, nurture them as they grow to become good citizens with a deeper relationship with God, and work with them in service to others.

> ***Train up a child in the way he should go: and when he is old,
> he will not depart from it.***
> ***—Proverbs 22:6 KJV***

Complete information relating to all of these awards is available through the Office of Civic Youth-Serving Agencies/Scouting at the General Commission on United Methodist Men in Nashville, Tennessee. (The brochures can be downloaded from www.umscouting.org.)

Affiliate Organizations

The United Methodist Men Foundation
The National Association of Conference Presidents founded the United
Methodist Men Foundation in 1981. The foundation was organized to

• operate exclusively for charitable and religious purposes
• provide support funds for program development and maintenance for the
  purpose and objectives of United Methodist Men.

The foundation has created endowments to fund a variety of United
Methodist Men ministries. Endowments help create financial security for
Christian programs and are a testimony by donors to the quality and worthi-
ness of the charitable organization receiving gifts. Endowments are our way
of providing for those who will follow in years to come.

The foundation first raised funds for scouting ministries. Gifts have helped
to keep a full-time staff person in scouting ministries for more than twenty-
five years. In addition, gifts have funded administrative costs of The Upper
Room Living Prayer Center, a toll-free telephone line, and numerous
national and international mission projects.

Gifts may be dedicated in honor or memory of a family member, friend, or
loved one. Endowment funds may be announced or they may be given
anonymously at the donor's discretion.

National Association of United Methodist Scouters
The purpose of the National Association of United Methodist Scouters
(NAUMS) is to enhance the outreach ministry of The United Methodist
Church to the children and youth of each church's community. Members
work with the Office of Civic Youth-Serving Agencies/Scouting (OCYSA/S)
in developing and promoting scouting as a ministry. For more information
please refer to the Organization Addresses section at the back of this book.

TRAINING
Each year the OCYSA/S holds a national training session for United
Methodist leaders at one of BSA's high-adventure bases. The Philmont
Training Center is part of Philmont Scout Ranch. It is located in Cimarron,
New Mexico, in the Sangre De Cristo mountain range. The setting provides
a relaxed atmosphere in which the scouting program of the Church may be
studied. Attendees are expected to return to their annual conferences, dis-
tricts, and local churches to conduct similar sessions for United Methodist
leaders. Another venue is the Florida Sea Base Conference and Retreat
Center in the Florida Keys. Other sites will be announced.

Resources

RESOURCES FROM THE OFFICE OF CIVIC YOUTH-SERVING AGENCIES/SCOUTING

To access resources and training material and/or training events, visit www.gcumm.org (Scouting Ministry) for current information.

Brochures and Packets
- "Benefits for Faith Communities" (Camp Fire USA: insert to *Community Family Club* brochure)
- *A Scout Is Reverent* (a BSA program publication about the BSA/UMC)
- *Bishop's Award of Excellence* (brochure)
- *The Cross and Flame Award* (brochure)
- *The Good Samaritan Award* (brochure)
- *Impact the Lives of Children and Youth in Our Communities* (brochure)
- *The Torch Award* (brochure)
- *The Silver Torch Award* (brochure)
- *The Shepherd Church Charter Recognition* (brochure)
- *UM Church/BSA: Building Values Together* (brochure)
- Civic Youth-Serving Agencies/Scouting (information packet)
- Guidelines for Organizing a Bishop's Dinner for Scouting (packet; DVD) (Limit 1 per order)
- Scouting Ministry (BSA) in The United Methodist Church (DVD)
- Training DVD (all-in-one)
- *Scouting Ministry Specialist* (brochure)

RESOURCES FROM COKESBURY
- *Guidelines for Leading Your Congregation: Scouting and Civic Youth-Serving Ministry,* 2013-2016.
- *The P.R.A.Y. Program* (This church program provides the basis for the P.R.A.Y. Award earned by members of the Boy Scouts of America, Girl Scouts of the USA, and Camp Fire USA. Includes four age levels: grades 1-3, grades 4-5, grades 6-8, and grades 9-12. Order through Cokesbury, 1-800-672-1789.)

RESOURCES FROM THE GENERAL COMMISSION ON UNITED METHODIST MEN
- *Strength for Service to God and Country* (Daily devotions for those in the service of others. Order through the website: www.strengthforservice.org; or from the publisher: www.cokesbury.com or call toll-free 1-800-672-1789. A Boy Scout edition is available from Cokesbury or at your local BSA Scout Shop.)

ORGANIZATION ADDRESSES

Big Brothers Big Sisters
230 North 13th Street
Philadelphia, PA 19107
www.bbbs.org

Boy Scouts of America
1325 Walnut Hill Lane
P.O. Box 152079
Irving, TX 75015-2079
Phone: (972) 580-2000
www.scouting.org

Camp Fire USA
1100 Walnut Street
Suite 1900
Kansas City, MO 64106-2197
Phone: (816) 285-2010
www.campfireusa.org

Girl Scouts of the USA
420 Fifth Avenue
New York, NY 10018
Phone: (212) 852-8000
www.girlscouts.org

Office of Civic Youth-Serving Agencies/Scouting
1000 17th Avenue South
Nashville, TN 37212
Phone: (615) 340-7145
Fax: (615) 340-1770
E-mail: lcoppock@gcumm.org
www.umscouting.org

P.R.A.Y.
11123 S. Towne Square, Suite B
St. Louis, MO 63123-7816
Phone: 800-933 PRAY (7729)
Fax: 314-845-0038
E-mail: info@praypub.org
www.praypub.org

National Association of United Methodist Scouters
P.O. Box 23172
Nashville, TN 37202-3172